Baby Cougar

By Beth Spanjian
Illustrated by Greg Beecham

A GOLDEN BOOK • NEW YORK
Western Publishing Company, Inc., Racine, Wisconsin 53404

Text © 1988 Angel Entertainment, Inc. Illustrations © 1988 Greg Beecham. All rights reserved. First published by Longmeadow Press.
Printed in the U.S.A. No part of this book may be reproduced or copied in any form without written permission from the publisher. GOLDEN,
GOLDEN & DESIGN, GOLDENCRAFT, A GOLDEN BOOK, A GOLDEN LOOK-LOOK BOOK, and A GOLDEN LOOK-LOOK BOOK & DESIGN
are trademarks of Western Publishing Company, Inc. Library of Congress Catalog Card Number: 90-81286   ISBN: 0-307-12597-1/
ISBN: 0-307-62597-4 (lib. bdg.)
MCMXCII

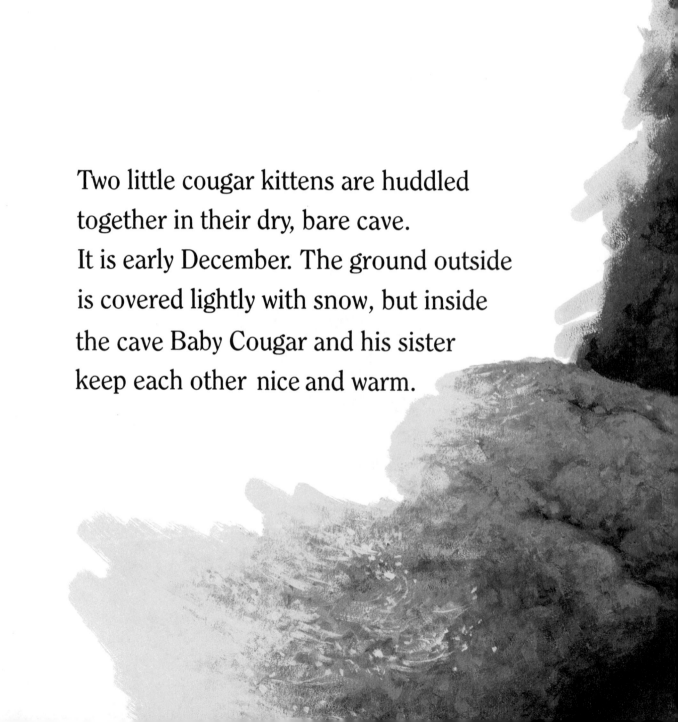

Two little cougar kittens are huddled
together in their dry, bare cave.
It is early December. The ground outside
is covered lightly with snow, but inside
the cave Baby Cougar and his sister
keep each other nice and warm.

The kittens yawn and stretch,
then wander out onto a sunny ledge.
The winter air feels cool and crisp.

Eager to play, the kittens scamper into the
nearby woods. Soon they find a large, clumsy
porcupine moving slowly along the ground.
Baby Cougar thinks he has found a new playmate!
When it sees Baby Cougar, the porcupine curls
into a big, black ball.

Baby Cougar strikes the porcupine with his quick, playful paw. Then he jumps back in surprise. His paw is full of sharp quills!

Mother Cougar is on her way home.
She has been hunting. The kittens
whimper when they hear her coming.
Their whimpers tell her they
are glad she is back.

The hunt was a success! Mother Cougar
leads the young ones to their breakfast.
Down the snowy slope they go, weaving in
and out of the mountain brush. The cougars
find a safe hiding place, where they can eat
in peace.

When they are finished eating, Mother Cougar
leads her kittens to a new den among the rocks.
She makes sure they are safe and warm.
Then she trots back to their eating spot,
to hide their food for the next day.

Suddenly, she hears the faint howl of hound dogs.
Mother Cougar knows that sound means trouble.
A hunter and his hounds are following her scent.
They are coming closer and closer.

Mother Cougar runs a short distance, then
leaps into an old, dead tree for safety.
She scurries up the tree, jumps onto a nearby cliff,
and disappears into the rocks. She has escaped!

Back at the den, Baby Cougar and his sister are playing near a rabbit hole. They see fresh rabbit tracks in the snow. The kittens crouch beside the dark hole, ready to pounce at anything that moves!

At the end of the day Mother Cougar comes
home, tired and panting. The kittens quickly
join her on the rocky ledge. Baby Cougar curls
up next to Mother Cougar. She gently licks his
soft fur with her tongue. By the time Baby
Cougar is all clean, he is fast asleep.

Facts About Baby Cougar

Where Do Cougars Live?

Cougars once roamed throughout the United States. Today they are extinct east of the Mississippi River, except for a few swamps in Florida. Over eighteen thousand cougars may exist in the United States. They are shy and secretive animals, rarely seen by people. Cougars live in the rocky, rugged brush country of the West's mountains and deserts, where deer and elk are plentiful.

What Do Cougars Eat?

Cougars are carnivores. This means that they eat mainly meat. Deer and elk make up a large part of their diet. Cougars quietly sneak up on their prey and catch it by surprise. The cats are very strong for their size and can easily leap twenty feet in one bound! Cougars also eat grass, porcupines, gophers, rabbits, ground squirrels and other animals.

How Do Cougars Communicate?

Cougars communicate by yowling, growling, hissing, whistling, whining, mewing and even purring. They also use body language, such as flattening their ears or showing their teeth when angry. Cougars will leave markings and small piles of dirt and brush called "scratch hills" along trails to let other cougars know they live nearby.

How Big Are Cougars, and How Long Do They Live?

Adult cougars weigh anywhere from eighty to two hundred pounds. Newborn kittens are only eight to twelve inches long, and weigh less than a pound. At eight weeks, the kittens may weigh ten pounds. A cougar of eight to twelve years is considered old, but some cougars have been known to live for as long as eighteen years.

What Is a Cougar's Family Like?

Mother cougars usually have twins and can have babies any time of the year. Litters range from one to six kittens. A mother cougar gives birth to her spotted kittens three months after breeding. The father cougar (called a tom) leaves the job of raising the kittens to the mother. She will take care of her young ones for nearly two years before they can fend for themselves.

What Is the Cougar's Future?

Cougars are now extinct from most of the United States. They were once considered a threat to deer and livestock herds, so game managers, ranchers and bounty hunters killed thousands of them. Recently, people have discovered that cougars are not so bad and help keep deer populations at healthy levels. Today, cougar numbers are slowly increasing. Laws control when, where and how hunters can kill them. Wildlife managers are now doing their best to keep cougars alive and well in the west.